In the Days

Zala Runs for Her Life

Story by Hugh Price
Illustrations by Michele Gaudion

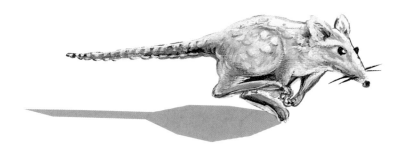

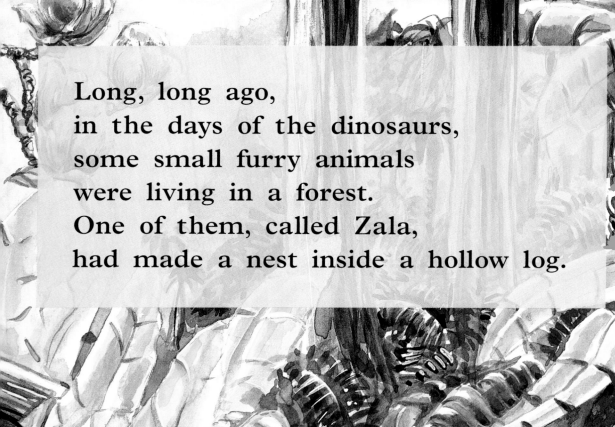

Long, long ago,
in the days of the dinosaurs,
some small furry animals
were living in a forest.
One of them, called Zala,
had made a nest inside a hollow log.

Zala had six very tiny babies.
At first they were pink,
because they had no fur,
and their eyes were tightly closed.
Zala fed them with her milk
and they grew quickly.

When the babies were two weeks old,
their fur had grown
and their eyes were open.
Now they could run around
inside the log.

They were sleepy in the daytime,
but at night, when Zala was out
hunting for insects,
they would run down to the end
of the log and look out.
They liked to smell **everything**
with their long noses.

5

Then, when the babies
were almost three weeks old,
Drome, the sharp-clawed dinosaur,
came looking for a meal.
He was only a small dinosaur,
but he was much
bigger than Zala,
and he was hungry.

Sniff, sniff! Scratch, scratch!
Zala and her babies woke up.

Sniff, sniff! Scratch, scratch!
They heard the scratching noises
coming nearer and nearer.

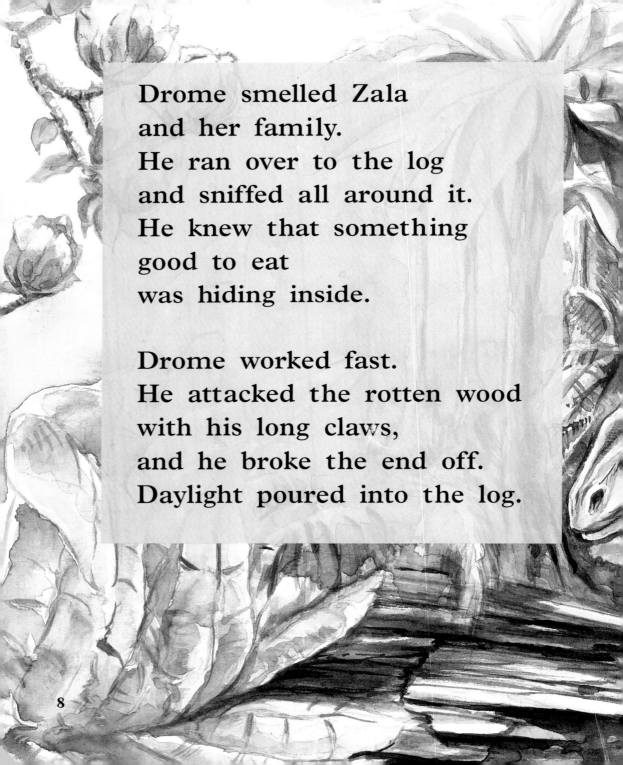

Drome smelled Zala
and her family.
He ran over to the log
and sniffed all around it.
He knew that something
good to eat
was hiding inside.

Drome worked fast.
He attacked the rotten wood
with his long claws,
and he broke the end off.
Daylight poured into the log.

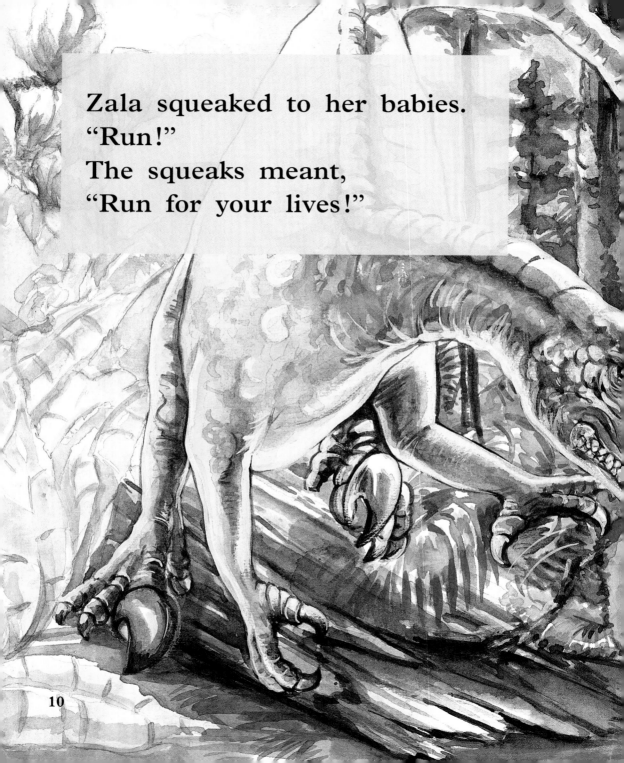

Zala squeaked to her babies.
"Run!"
The squeaks meant,
"Run for your lives!"

10

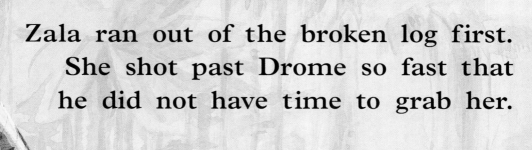

Zala ran out of the broken log first. She shot past Drome so fast that he did not have time to grab her.

She dashed under the ferns and crawled under a rock beside the roots of a tree. Drome raked the ground with his claws, but he could not see where she had gone. Zala was safe!

As soon as their mother squeaked
and raced out of the log,
the six tiny babies ran for cover, too.
Some ran one way
and some ran another.
They hid down among
the leaves and roots
on the forest floor.

Drome tore the nest to pieces
with his huge claws,
but all that was left inside the log
was the smell of Zala's family.

Drome sniffed crossly
as he went away.
He would have to look
for something else to eat.

When Drome had gone,
Zala came out from under the rock
and called to her babies.

They all heard her calls
and came running to join her.
They were cold and shaking with fright.
Zala fed them and licked them clean.

Then she led her family
deep into the forest
where the trees grew close together.
Zala found another hole to hide in.
And there they all stayed
until the little ones were big enough
to catch insects for themselves.